BIRMINGHAM AND THE BLACK COUNTRY MURDER STORIES

RECALLING THE EVENTS OF SOME OF THE MOST
WELL-KNOWN MURDERS IN BIRMINGHAM AND
THE BLACK COUNTRY

Brendan Hawthorne

BRADWELL
BOOKS

Published by Bradwell Books

9 Orgreave Close Sheffield S13 9NP

Email: books@bradwellbooks.co.uk

1st Edition

ISBN: 9781910551967

Print: Gomer Press, Llandysul, Ceredigion SA44 4JL

Artwork by: Andrew Caffrey

Photograph Credits: Images credited individually

ACKNOWLEDGEMENTS

Thanks to Lynn, my wife, for listening to the
strange dreams I had whilst compiling this book!

A big 'thank you' to the staff, John, Gavin and Dan,
at *The Black Country Bugle* who allowed me access
to their archive material.

Thanks also to Peggy & Kev and to Roy for
their continued interest and to Ian Bott, a fellow
researcher, for his kindness.

CONTENTS

INTRODUCTION

The true murders and attempted murders portrayed in this book all took place within the boundaries of the industrial heartlands of Birmingham and the Black Country.

Many publications and newspaper articles already exist reporting on and presenting findings of this region's well-documented but brutal social history. As an author, I have taken some of the more well-known and other lesser-known stories and re-presented them to you, dear reader, but keeping strictly to the recorded courtroom facts to remain true to the original story. In this region, many crimes were committed against a backdrop of poverty, filth and lifestyles of drudgery and drink. Low pay and poor socio-economic and sanitary conditions from the dawn of industrialisation to the slum clearances of the 1930s laid the path to many foul crimes. This is not to excuse anyone or assuage guilt in any way but merely sets the individual cases against the conditions of adversity that, for many people, was their uncontrollable lot.

Here we go then! From would-be poisoners to murders over money and affairs of the heart, this book will give you an introduction to some of the stories that end up behind bars or with the hangman's rope. Whether a means of introduction to further personal research or a journey into the region's gruesome past then this is the book for you.

READ ON IF YOU DARE. Beware the month of July and BE WARNED: if you read late at night you may need to sleep with the light on!

A FRENZIED RAZOR ATTACK IN STOURBRIDGE

THIS STORY TURNS THE CLOCK BACK TO THE INTER-WAR YEAR OF 1925 AND TO STOURBRIDGE, A BLACK COUNTRY TOWN WITH A PROUD INDUSTRIAL HERITAGE AND A COURTROOM READY TO DISPATCH THOSE GUILTY OF CRIME TO MEET THEIR FATE AT THE SHIRE ASSIZES. STEP INTO THE DOCK A VIOLENT BRICKLAYER'S LABOURER FROM NEARBY LYE.

This story of a 'feeble-minded' young man and his love for his stepsister was heard on 10 July 1925 at Stourbridge Police Court. The 23-year-old man stood accused of inflicting more than forty wounds to Alice Mary Rowley for simply not returning his attentions. In the 11 July 1925 edition of *the Birmingham Gazette* this whole sorry story of Bert Checketts of Stourbridge Road was unfolded for public consumption. Checketts had been working as a bricklayer's labourer and had a reported history of violent outbursts. He was not considered to be of mortal danger to either himself or to others by family and friends, although he was deemed to be a man you wouldn't cross.

The case had initially been brought to the attention of Alderman Selleck at Stourbridge on 8 July when the accused was remanded. It was noted that the accused stood without any apparent knowledge of the seriousness of his charges and seemed indifferent to the accusations on which he would be judged.

His stepsister Mary, as she was known, had made the fatal mistake of resisting his physical demands and quarrelling over a silver sixpence. Witnesses said that an argument had occurred between Checketts and his stepsister on the previous Saturday night following an earlier dispute over a sixpence loan, over which Checketts continued to hold a grudge. It was observed that she appeared afraid as she resisted both his menacing behaviour and the physical advances being made by him. On the evening of the murder screams and shouting had been heard coming from the shared property where they lived. This was followed by a long silence.

A neighbour, Mrs Pardoe, saw Checketts smeared in blood standing outside the gate to the property. The lifeless body of Mary lay but a few yards away. Another passing witness, Mr Saywell, told Mrs Pardoe that the dead woman had had her throat cut and her clothing was completely saturated in blood from multiple wounds to the whole of her body. But Checketts protested that she had done it to herself. In court his protests continued and he went on to accuse his victim of injuring his hand. *'Look how she served me!'* he said, showing his injury to those present. Mary's mother reported that the accused had been acting 'oddly' of late.

The post-mortem confirmed that between forty and fifty 'incisive' wounds had been inflicted upon Mary and concluded that death had been caused through shock and blood loss from the wounds to her neck and throat. It was further concluded that these wounds could not have been self-inflicted but had been delivered, with force, by someone attacking her from behind before furthering the attack. The accused, however, told police that the girl had taken a razor from a drawer and then went outside to injure herself. He said he followed her outside to stop her from doing so, at which point a struggle ensued.

Checketts' own father said that his son had stalked his victim when she went out for a walk, that her clothes had been wilfully damaged at home and that some of her hats had been taken outside and buried in what must have been an attempt to keep her indoors and under his son's control.

Twenty-two-year-old Mary was buried on 9 July at Lye,

where massive crowds had gathered to see the poor unfortunate committed to an early grave, her mother being reported as being too ill to attend.

So what of Checketts? A simple individual, described in the press as neither imbecile, idiot nor criminally insane, but who wanted to possess his stepsister and in the end, it seems, murdered her for not submitting to his forceful whims.

'The Mitre' public house in Stourbridge is sited at the hub of the town.
Creative Commons PL Chadwick

The trial took place on 23 October at Worcester Assizes, where Checketts submitted a plea of not guilty on the grounds of insanity. This plea seemed at odds with the graphic evidence that appeared both in the press and at the hearing and which seemed to prove that this was a frenzied attack on a defenceless young woman. The sentence of death by hanging was in the end reduced to one of life imprisonment, where Checketts would have been held in some secure prison wing.

It is here that this story remains open to theory and some conjecture. What is fact, however, is that a young woman was killed in the act of self-defence. Whether the attack was pre-meditated or on the grounds of insanity did not change the outcome of her fate on that July evening in 1925.

LOVE'S FAILED LEAP OF THE POVERTY GAP

THE OLD SAYING THAT ONE CANNOT LIVE ON LOVE ALONE LENDS EVEN MORE POIGNANCY TO THIS SAD STORY. THE ATTEMPT OF TWO LOVERS TO MAKE SOMETHING OF THEMSELVES LED TO AN INCIDENT OF MURDEROUS PATHOS WHEN TRYING TO ESCAPE THE HUNGRY MOUTH OF STARVATION.

The area of Aston houses a Domesday Manor and a major football ground and gives its name to an expressway that forms part of the restless tangle of roads serving and ringing the city of Birmingham. The River Tame runs close by, as well as the interchange of canals that served Victorian industries. Double-decker trams would have once rumbled along, carrying those who could afford the fare to their chosen destinations.

Sitting close to a major industrial area, Aston saw both the very rich and the very poor collide on streets that told tales of both hardship and fortune. One young couple in their late teens could only dream of making something of themselves on the cobbled streets of Brum. In the midsummer of 1911 this particular couple waited for their love to bloom after twelve months of stepping out. Instead, it died upon the vine.

The River Tame runs through Witton and makes its way unseen under the motorway interchange today. Creative Commons John M

Sarah found work in any job to which she could apply herself. Long hours and low pay could not sustain her and her out-of-work partner, Thomas. They dreamed and planned as lovers do, but their fate would not allow them to take their relationship any further. They had planned to run away from their pitiful existence in Phillips Street and together find a new life. Unfortunately, it led them only to a transient lifestyle, stumbling from one bout of poverty to another.

Their situation went from bad to worse, so much so that Sarah started to pawn what clothing and jewellery she had left just to feed their empty stomachs. Occasionally they could afford shelter instead of sleeping rough. It appears that Thomas either had nothing left to give or was more reluctant than Sarah to part with what little he had.

With the meagre proceeds of Sarah's sales, they spent their money at a hostelry in Witton, a couple of miles from Aston, where a member of staff overheard accusations being made by Thomas that Sarah had been unfaithful to him. In those times it wasn't uncommon for women to sell a little more of themselves than jewellery and dabble in the oldest profession, prostitution. They had to admit that their lifestyle was now leading them to the doors of the poorhouse. They slept rough again that night, under the veranda of a sports club. This was to be the last night of dreams for Sarah. Her body was found the next day close to the cricket club, her blouse raised and a knife plunged into her chest.

Thomas went on the run for two days, abandoning his sweetheart. Finally he gave himself up to a policeman and admitted his crime. After confessing to the police and to his visiting mother, Thomas pleaded not guilty in court and put forward the scenario that he and Sarah had planned a double suicide. She had placed the knife to her own chest and slipped the blade into her flesh before one last kiss. However, a doctor refuted this tale as the knife had been forced into her body and he concluded that Sarah had not been standing when the fatal wound was inflicted.

So was that last treat at a Witton hostelry the final meal they had planned together? Was the suicide pact a serious one up until the point of delivery? Did Thomas falter and decide to put Sarah out of her misery in a final act of misplaced love? All of this conjecture only leads us to what went on in the courtroom on the day of sentencing. Despite repeated outpourings of Thomas's claims of innocence, the jury gave their guilty verdict to the courtroom as the lights went out in a final act of drama.

The judge gave his verdict by candlelight: one of death by hanging. A mercy plea was accepted, however, and Thomas spent the rest of his life in prison, once more a verdict commuted to a lesser charge on the grounds of living a pitiful life. Sarah's sentence, however, was unredeemable.

A VERY POISONOUS PEN

THE ERDINGTON NEWS OF 30TH JULY 1927 REPORTED ON A VERY STRANGE 'MURDER', IF INDEED ONE MURDER CAN BE STRANGER THAN ANOTHER. THERE WAS NO PHYSICAL WEAPON, NO DIRECT ASSAILANT AND NO PHYSICAL WITNESS. HOWEVER, LETTERS THAT WERE FOUND SPOKE LOUDLY AND CLEARLY OF THE CIRCUMSTANCES THAT LED TO THE UNTIMELY DEATH OF A YOUNG WORKING-CLASS WOMAN.

Twenty-six-year-old Nancy Derrick, a domestic servant, was found dead in the Birmingham Canal at Tower Hill, Great Barr, which lies just to the north of the city. To all intents and purposes, it looked like just another suicide claimed by the canal network that had become such a convenient way to make a living – or a killing. However, on further inspection of the facts, it was soon clear that the reason for this sad loss of a young life was far from simple, for the instrument of death, it seems, was nothing more than the poison contained in a pen.

Mr Frank Cooper, a coroner from South Staffordshire, summed up his findings by directing his comments to the young plasterer who stood in front of him, William

Lockwood Jnr, of 57 Platt Street, Hednesford: *'The law of England, very fortunately for you, does not make you criminally responsible for this girl's death, but morally you are as responsible for Nancy Derrick's death as many a man who has been hanged for murder.'*

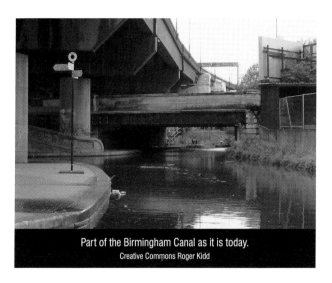

Part of the Birmingham Canal as it is today.
Creative Commons Roger Kidd

Strong and accusatory words, which must have carved through the silence in the air at the inquest. The sequence of events that led to this statement is as strange as the cornoner's concluding remarks.

Nancy had been working as a domestic servant at Gravelly House, Gravelly Hill (in the vicinity of the place many of you will have inadvertently experienced in more recent times as the Gravelly Hill interchange, better known as Spaghetti Junction). A note was left for her mistress following Nancy's disappearance that told of her personal situation prior to death. She told her that she had loved and lost and could see no other way out than this. The letters she had left behind in her suitcase, she said, were the cause of all of her suffering.

Will's father had promised to help the young couple if she 'gave in for the loved one' – his son. Once she had told Mr Lockwood of her acquiescence and compliance, however, he ignored her for a time, as his son was in fact already married. Loyal to the end, she swore her love to Will, who initially she had been led to believe was a single man, and hoped he wouldn't be blamed for anything.

Forty-six-year-old William Lockwood of Cannock said he had asked the girl about his son's relationship with her and she had said that they were merely friends. However, this did not stop William Lockwood Senior trying to console the young lady with his own smooth banter when trying to ease the pain of her losing communication with his son.

The story of the older William continues through several letters in his own hand, where on one occasion, after a meeting had been arranged, he asks the young lady not to speak to him as his own wife would be there. He signed his letters with *'Best love and kisses'*! The coroner asked him if this was appropriate in the light of this young lady coming between his son and daughter-in-law. He also found in another letter that Lockwood Snr had asked for her to remain *'with the one always thinking about her'*, unquestionably meaning himself.

The inquest then added one more fact: that Nancy had been found to be pregnant. The coroner said that he had no doubt it was William Jnr's child and could not believe for one minute from the evidence that his claim of having had nothing to do with her was true. William Jnr had up until this point been living a happy family life with his own wife and child but was accused at the inquest of deserting the young lady when he found out she was pregnant.

Both father and son had led a young girl of good moral standing to a cold and watery end. She took her own life and that of the unborn child and a verdict of 'suicide of unsound mind' was returned. Frank Cooper, however, would not be swayed in his contempt for the Lockwoods, a stigma attached so forcibly that they would arguably never have escaped its taint.

WASTELAND MURDER OF INNOCENT MARY

THE HEINOUS CRIME OF MURDER IS OFTEN THE RESULT OF THE DESIRE OF ONE PERSON TO CONTROL ANOTHER, TAKEN TO EXTREME ENDS. WHEN ONE PERSON'S ATTENTION IS NOT REQUITED OR THEIR VIEW RECOGNISED THE LEVEL OF FRUSTRATION AND NEED WITHIN THE PSYCHE OF THE PERPETRATOR CAN CRACK AN ALREADY FRACTURED STATE OF MIND INTO A MOOD OF FRENZY – SOMETHING THAT LED TO THE REPEAL OF AN ANCIENT LAW.

The morning of 27th May 1817 began uneventfully for labourer, George Jackson. Setting off on his daily ten-mile walk from his home in Hurst Street, Birmingham, to his Sutton Coldfield workplace, he passed all the usual sights and scenes; only the weather and the seasons changed. He walked along Moor Street, heard the parish clock chime five a.m. and, passing the workhouse, he continued along Bell Lane and off onto a pathway to the old water-filled pit on the edge of a marshy clover field. But on this particular morning, to the side of the pit opening, he observed a pile of bloodstained clothing.

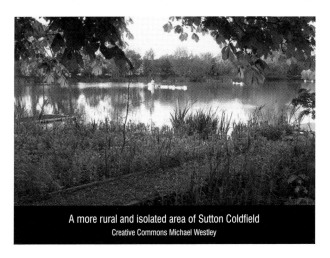

A more rural and isolated area of Sutton Coldfield
Creative Commons Michael Westley

George ran to a nearby house shouting for help. The occupier, William Lavell, agreed to accompany him back to the pile of clothes. George ran on to get more help from a nearby wire factory, where some of the workforce came out to help search the area. James Simmons dragged the pit with equipment he had brought with him just in case of need and by eight a.m. he had recovered the body of twenty-year-old Mary Ashford, a local woman.

The soft field of clover lay witness to the sequence of events and pretty soon it was evident that she had been chased, attacked and then dumped into the pit. A single set of footprints left the field in the direction of Castle Bromwich.

Mary's body was taken to the Lavells' house where Mrs Lavell and another local woman carefully undressed her. There was clear evidence that a struggle had taken place from bruising to the arms, and further layers of bloodstained clothing revealed injuries to the lower body.

The police acted upon witness statements and promptly arrested Abraham Thornton on suspicion of murder. Thornton, a Castle Bromwich bricklayer, was the last person seen with Mary and this gave them initial grounds for his arrest. The post-mortem subsequently revealed that she had been alive when she was thrown into the pit and had not died from her injuries but had in fact drowned.

The evening that led to Mary's demise started at a local feast day dance. Accompanied by her female friend, she had been excited at the prospect of this local custom. Mary's morals and lifestyle were reported to have been exemplary and although from a poor Langley family she was honest with good intentions. Thornton proceeded to take advantage of her company throughout the evening, beginning to make advances and, when rebuked, remarked that her sister had been more willing to make his acquaintance. He told her that she would yield, even it cost him his own life.

Mary left to return home with Thornton still at her side. At three a.m. both Mary and Thornton were seen at a stile and at four a.m. Mary stopped by at a friend's house in Erdington to get changed, where she seemed in good spirits and was carrying a bundle of clothes. It can be assumed that around the time George Jackson was leaving Hurst Street to go to work, Mary's life was about to face its violent and sad end at the hands and desires of Thornton.

Hurst Street Creative Commons Brian-Robert-Marshally

Witness accounts matched the timeline of events, as work had started early on the land that morning with sunrise being in the early hours. Further investigation led to Thornton's shoes being matched to the imprints left in the clover field. As the evidence unfolded it was clear that Thornton's defence rested on there being a mutual desire between Mary and Thornton and his claim that Mary, in a fit of remorse and guilt, threw herself into the pit.

The case was not proven and witness evidence heavily relied on rough estimates of time to pull the facts together in a cohesive timeline. It was on this basis and because all the evidence was circumstantial that the trial ended in an acquittal, to great public outrage; some, no doubt, from those who felt cheated of a hanging.

Relatives and friends of Mary would not give up on getting justice and it did not rest easily with them that her name had been dragged through the press. The Revd Luke Booker, Vicar of Dudley, added his voice to the outcry and soon the people evoked an application of the then law of 'Appeal of Murder'. The Writ of Appeal was received by the Sheriff of Warwick on 10 October, demanding the re-arrest of Thornton in connection with the murder of Mary. The court case finally re-opened on 17 November, when, to a crowded Warwick Assizes, Thornton again pleaded not guilty and stated that he would claim his innocence under the lawful rights of 'Trial by Combat', where God would finally decide his fate and his innocence, a system of legal outcome initially employed in the Middle Ages.

It took until 16 April 1818 for the judges to decide that if Mary's father, Mr Ashford, could place his antiquated 'Appeal of Murder' into a courtroom then, by the same rights, Thornton could request the equally antiquated 'Trial by Combat'. Four days later Mr Ashford withdrew his request, leaving Abraham Thornton a free man. Thornton was so hated locally that he decided to emigrate to America, but when hie first booked his passage no one would sail with him. Eventually Thornton sailed out of Liverpool on the Shamrock.

It was subsequently claimed that Thornton had left behind a note giving his version of what happened on that May evening in 1817. It came into the possession of a Liverpool prostitute, who passed it on to Birmingham police. In the letter, Thornton admitted attacking Mary in such a way that if she accused him of it he would hang. He admitted carrying her to the pit and throwing her into it. However, the letter was later found to be fake. Many rumours circulated as to the whereabouts and death of Thornton but nothing was ever proven as to their accuracy. Birmingham writer George Ludlum wrote a play based on the case the same year: *Mysterious Murder*, or, *What's the Clock?* Trial by Combat was abolished in law in 1819.

THE MURDEOUS BRUMMY ROUGHS

SQUALID SOCIAL CONDITIONS, LIFE-OR-DEATH NEEDS AND LOW EXPECTATION INGRAINED CRIME INTO GENERATIONS OF PEOPLE LIVING THEIR PITIFULLY SHORT LIVES ON THE BACK STREETS OF BIRMINGHAM. SAFETY IN NUMBERS WAS THE USUAL APPROACH TO PERSONAL SECURITY, WHICH LED TO GANGS SETTING THEMSELVES UP AGAINST EACH OTHER TO GAIN FIRST DABS ON A RICH OR GULLIBLE PERSON'S POCKETS. BUT ALL TOO OFTEN THOSE PICKINGS ULTIMATELY LED ONLY TO THE HAZY RECOLLECTIONS OF ALCOHOL-FUELLED TIRADES OF FORCE.

Life imprisonment was welcomed as a merciful release for some, and one young lady who had seen much in the way of hard living and regular beatings sought revenge, knowing it would mean her spending only a short time longer on this earth. She had been pushed to a point where she could no longer face her lot in the company of 'Brummy Roughs' and, in particular, one man: the one she was currently living with.

Not far from the newly re-developed Bullring Shopping Centre and concert arenas in Birmingham there once lay an area of poverty and squalor. Leopold Street was a very poor area at the turn of the twentieth century. Crowded living conditions and poverty created breaking-point situations and as in many other areas of the city people were barely clinging to existence.

Leopold Street as it looks in more recent times of redevelopment
Creative Commons Chris Whippet

Fanny Williams was married but now found herself living with James Higgins and his mother. Fanny worked in low-paid, low-skilled jobs for long hours and when she wasn't working her fingers to the bone she was being beaten by her new-found love. Fanny had left her home and Higgins couldn't be charged with wife-beating as they weren't married. The law provided little comfort for couples who were co-habiting.

Fanny became a hardened drinker to soften the harsh reality of her life and one night in September 1911, returning from the pub with her equally inebriated partner, her temper literally became incandescent. Earlier, Higgins' mother had bought paraffin for the oil lamps and left the liquid, handily for Fanny, in the hallway. Higgins slumped in a chair by a table, ordering Fanny to remove his boots. He lashed out with his hobnails and so Fanny rebelliously obliged. This she did with liberal amounts of paraffin splashed about his person and the application of a match!

Higgins' brother returned an hour later to the stinging smell of smoke and burning coming from his family home, only to see his brother ablaze at the table and to find Fanny huddled in a corner of the wash/brew house with a bottle of beer to hand. Her victim died at the local hospital a few hours later, succumbing to the awful burns that covered his body.

Florence 'Fanny' Williams, in a statement to the police, admitted her crime. Her admission could only realistically lead her to the gallows but that held no fear for her. In fact, she repeated that she would do it again and face the same consequences for her actions. In December of that year she faced a murder charge.

Her defence of pre-existing conditions of epilepsy and alcohol-driven temper led to witness statements that could have made her actions seem to be the only rational thing to do in the circumstances. Unfortunately, this only served to annoy the judge and, it seemed, Fanny herself. All the evidence and doctors; reports made while she was on remand were swept aside by her sticking to her truth and her self-confessed guilt. She knew her fate and appeared to just want to get on and face it. Even when the judge in his summing up mentioned 'mercy', Fanny retorted that she wanted none.

The jury took only half an hour to return a verdict of guilty. The death sentence was duly passed, but before leaving court Fanny gave a statement that seemed to put into context the type of life she and her peers endured. It can be interpreted from this statement that her personal life and working life had offered little comfort to her over the years, living on meagre rations and uncertain as to where the next meal was coming from, whereas her time in prison had allowed her to make friends and had given some relative comfort and security at a time when she had none.

Fanny was imprisoned at Winson Green and awaited news of the noose. However, three weeks later she had her sentence reduced to one of life imprisonment. Maybe this was seen at the time as not giving a guilty prisoner what they wanted with a merciful release from this world. It also offered a legal sense of mercy in extenuating circumstances, taking into account that the accused had shown signs of epileptic seizure. Maybe life imprisonment would have been recognised as a greater punishment to her for the horrendous method of revenge that became known as 'The Leopold Street Murder'.

We may never know the reasoning but it appears that Fanny was happy in the knowledge that her final resting place, whenever that might be, would be contained within the security of a prison wall.

THE WOULD-BE 'CONDIMENT' POISONER OF BILSTON

iStock

THIS SECOND VISIT TO JULY 1925 UNCOVERS A PLOT BY AN ESTRANGED WIFE AND HER LOVER TO REMOVE THE OBSTACLE THAT HAD BEEN LEFT BETWEEN THEM AND THEIR NEW-FOUND LOVE: HER HUSBAND! TAKING ADVICE THROUGH LOVE LETTERS, BILSTON'S DOROTHY HENSHAW FACED TRIAL FOR AN ATTEMPTED POISONING, THE DETAILS OF WHICH BECAME MORE ABSURD AND BIZARRE AS THE CASE PROCEEDED.

You can almost hear the newspaper sellers calling, *'Would-be food poisoners get their just desserts! Laundry bleach, laudanum or gas?!'* A spot on his dinner of the former would do it, that or a whiff of the latter.

A strange cocktail of lust and conspiracy to murder led a migrant Irish worker, forty-one-year-old plasterer Alexander Pelan, to aid and abet his younger collaborator, thirty-five-year-old Dorothy Henshaw of Bilston. Their mutual desire for each other led to an alleged plot to kill Henshaw's husband to get him 'out of the way'.

On 1st July Staffordshire Assizes heard how disgusting letters of carnal and murderous intent had passed between the two prisoners who now stood trial. Mrs Henshaw's husband dramatically refused to give evidence when called upon at the trial but wasn't allowed to stand down. At this, Mrs Henshaw broke down. Clearly, the husband at this point was unaware of the criminal intentions or romantic leanings of his wife and the man who was once their short-term lodger.

The letters themselves came to light through the censorship of mail to and from Ireland at the time of the couple's planned affair. Censorship was put in place to keep faithful followers of the Catholic Church 'pure of thought' and to protect them from outside influences of an unholy nature. However, it was Pelan who initially suggested bleach, laudanum or gas as a solution to the frustrated couple not being able to spend more time together. A returning letter from Mrs Henshaw told of her going out after putting a 'spot' of something on her husband's food, but on her return she had found no effect. In fact, her husband had neither complained nor commented on the addition to his meal and seemed totally unperturbed by its inclusion. Pelan suggested that maybe the spot wasn't enough, but they concluded that too much would 'find them out'.

It appears from the content of the letters from Henshaw to Pelan that she lived a life she could no longer bear, possibly one of perceived drudgery. Pelan had clearly given her a sense of excitement in her life for the brief time they were in other's company, the last time being Christmas 1924. Henshaw bitterly concluded that she wished she wasn't nursing the children through their illnesses but nursing her husband through his lethal ingestion instead. Henshaw put her failure in dealing with her husband down to needing more days to poison him, and if she was in a position of nursing him, she would, she said, *'Put him through it'*.

When confronted, Pelan denied all knowledge of the conspiracy and claimed that the letters were merely a concoction. He added that he had stayed with the family over twelve months previously and that he knew the couple that way. Henshaw denied giving her husband anything to poison him but on cross-examination at the trial a bottle of 'salt of lemon' sent by Pelan was produced as evidence. Salt of lemon was used as a stain remover or bleach and could cause stomach irritation or heart failure if taken internally and in some quantity, and was therefore a domestic poison. Henshaw denied that her actions were potentially poisonous. Pelan went on to say that none of the letters were meaningful and what she did was a thoughtless thing to have done. Henshaw said pretty much the same thing. The judge, on reflection, called them a *'miserable pair'*, added that they weren't worth severely punishing and went on to call them *'wretched specimens'*.

The judge's words about Pelan and Henshaw are recorded in the *Birmingham Gazette*, as are their sentences. Both defendants were found guilty of conspiracy and sentenced accordingly and proportionately. Pelan was sentenced to fifteen months' hard labour and Henshaw to nine months' hard labour. These sentences were no doubt based on the old Victorian principles that idle hands and minds can conspire to mischief and that hard manual enforced labour would 're-educate' the unfortunate. Reading between the lines, and considering that ultimately no harm was done, the sentence in modern-day parlance would be nothing more than a community service order!

Their labourings and their ultimate freedom aren't documented but their embarrassment and punishment were very public. It is not known whether they ever contacted each other again but the outcome of this romantic dalliance would have taught these would-be poisoners a valuable lesson in the art of social intercourse!

ASYLUM ROAD SURGEON ATTENDS VICTIM OF BAKER'S SICKENING ATTACK

GEORGE NICHOLSON, A WIDOWER AND TRAVELLING BAKER, UNHAPPILY SETTLED IN BIRMINGHAM LOOKING FOR WORK BUT FOUND ONLY THE DEEP UNHAPPINESS THAT LED TO THE BRUTAL MURDER OF HIS SECOND WIFE AS SHE SAT IN THE KITCHEN ROCKING CHAIR, CALMING HERSELF FROM YET ANOTHER ARGUMENT OVER MONEY.

The September of 1888 saw Burlington Road, Potters Hill, Birmingham become the centre of attention for all the wrong reasons. Martha Wark, on hearing an argument in the neighbouring property, became concerned for the woman next door and her grown-up children. She heard a loud snoring sound after the argument had abated. She later realised that these were the last dying breaths of a murder victim.

Burlington Street lies between Newtown and Aston and is now a fairly recently re-developed area of the city. In 1888 cramped and crowded conditions would as usual have led to pressure building over finances and lifestyle. Saturday 22nd September must have been like any other day for Mary Ann Nicholson, wife of George. Mrs Nicholson, aged fifty-two, had four children by a previous marriage, three of whom still resided with her, those being Mary Ann, Albert and Prudence Eccleston, who all had to give their version of events alongside neighbours and work colleagues at the trial of their stepfather in determining whether the crime had been committed by an intruder or in fact by George Nicholson himself.

That fateful morning Nicholson, a journeyman baker, went to work with some cooked food at 4.45 a.m., where he said to fellow baker Henry Townsend that the food had caused a row between him and his wife and that he could do a 'Whitechapel on them.' Nicholson was obsessed by the recent Whitechapel murders and seemed to be referring to how he felt about his wife and her family.

During that evening a row broke out between husband and wife regarding a short payment of one shilling and sixpence instead of the full two shillings, which Mrs Nicholson was demanding from her husband for lodgings, an arrangement acceptable to both parties. Neighbours heard a chair being thrown and George Nicholson banging out of the back door from the kitchen, where raised voices had been heard earlier. Albert and Mary Ann had not long left from visiting their mother and were soon called back to see if everything was all right at the house. The two young people were greeted with their mother sitting in a rocking chair holding her head, which was streaming with blood. Albert ran for the local surgeon. Dr Vincent Jones from Asylum Road was called to assist the poor lady. He soon deduced that the fatal wounds to the head had been caused by a coal axe or hatchet, later found with the victim's blood and matted hair still attached to it. Several blows had been administered from behind with great force. By the time the doctor arrived life was already extinct.

Witness evidence placed George Nicholson at the time and place of the murder around nine and ten p.m. He heard witness statements saying that he had indeed threatened to kill his wife during the unhappy three months at Burlington Road. He was heard walking across the back yard after burying the axe in his wife's head, having taken it from a cupboard in the scullery, but the most damning evidence of all was that of a bloodstained watch and chain which had been pledged at Benjamin Rubenstein's pawnbrokers on Newtown

Row, a watch that was still warm from the victim's body. Mr Rubenstein said he was disturbed by appearance and mannerisms of the customer, who gave the name of George Harrison for the claim ticket, number 113. He also gave a false address. Nicholson asked for 25 shillings but was offered a sovereign for the silver watch and gold chain. After a brief discussion the offer was raised by three shillings, which was accepted.

Nicholson, a widower, was described as a pale, thin man with a broad hump on his back and, although new to the locale, was already well known by sight and manner. After leaving Rubenstein's, he caught a late train to Walsall, a town where he had once lived. He was clearly trying to find shelter in an environment he knew well. Unfortunately for him it was where the police finally picked him up the following day, still in his bloodstained clothes. Sergeant Parker and Superintendent Walker took him to Aston police station where locals identified him as George Nicholson.

Nicholson later informed Detective Inspector Winkless that he had had a lot to drink the night before and could hardly remember how he had arrived in Walsall other than getting on the train. The possibility that his wife had committed suicide was discussed but all the evidence and witness statements placed the blame for wilful murder on Nicholson himself. He pleaded not guilty to murder and was detained at Winson Green awaiting his time in the dock at Worcester Assizes, where on 17th December the evidence would be judged to determine his fate. He was inevitably found guilty of murder and sentenced to face his own death at the hands of the executioner.

Winson Green Prison Creative Commons

CONTRACT KILLING AT ETTINGSHALL?

A LIFELESS BODY FOUND ON WASTELAND IN 1914 LED TO THE ASSUMPTION THAT AN EXECUTION HAD TAKEN PLACE. IT HAD THE HALLMARKS OF A CRIME NOT USUALLY KNOWN IN THE NORTHERN PART OF THE BLACK COUNTRY AND RAISED MORE QUESTIONS THAN ANSWERS IN THIS VERY STRANGE CASE OF COLD-BLOODED MURDER.

Ettingshall is an industrial area that lies between Bilston and Wolverhampton. Many steel factories reached up to the skies with their smokestacks and polluted the air with the acrid notes of industry. On 20th January 1914 there emerged a case that police couldn't solve. Neither could they get to the bottom of the complex web of intrigue that emerged about the victim and the person who last saw him alive. Just how did an Australian-born American ship's engineer meet his last moments on this earth and have his remains left propped against a brick wall with his eyes weeping blood?

Only three days earlier, Kent Reeks had landed at

Liverpool docks from Boston in the USA to book his final ticket with fate. *The Black Country Bugle* featured this strange case in October 1991, one that still retains a much-vexed conclusion.

In the early twentieth century many people took to well-trodden tracks and canal towpaths as local routes to take breakfast to family members working in nearby factories. On the morning of 20th January 1914 one young girl was walking to Wright's Foundry with some 'snap' for a relative who worked in the heavy and dirty industry there. Her routine journey took her across 'tocky' (clay spoil from mining) dirt and larger spoil mounds, eventually passing an old disused pit-shaft before Wright's came into easy walking distance. It was here that her routine journey came to a shocking and abrupt halt.

Sitting with his back to the circular wall she noticed what appeared to be a drunk sleeping off the excesses of the night before. She walked quietly around, not wanting to disturb him and, as in most cases with a disgruntled drunk, she didn't want to wake his temper either. However, she did gingerly creep over towards the man to see if she recognised him and, indeed, if he was all right. In the half-light of early morning, she peered and gazed in horror when staring into the man's face – for he had no eyes! Blood had run down his cheeks, his features chiselled with shock and horror. His blackened eye sockets and bloody forehead suggested that this was no drunk or even the victim of a drunken brawl. This was far more sinister than anything she had ever seen.

The young girl let out screams that were heard by local workmen. They quickly ran to her aid and through the mist they too saw the horrors she had witnessed. A local bobby was called for, who quickly passed the findings on to a more senior police officer. Who was this unfortunate victim of such a horrendous attack?

In the victim's pockets a re-directed letter gave some idea of who he was and where he was from, as well as where he had been only the day before. Robbery was ruled out as a motive, due to money being found in his wallet, and the victim was officially identified later by his uncle, who lived in Manchester and told police that his nephew had visited him only a few days earlier. He had noticed that he was carrying a substantial amount of American money, so had he been robbed? Was the murder a needs-based robbery after all?

Kent, or E.S. Hyde as he was also known, had, it seemed, met another man whom police could not trace. A Mr Ramsden, also American, had signed into the same hotel as Kent and then disappeared. Local stories told of two 'Yanks' drinking whisky in a local pub and behaving oddly. They had even left the premises without finishing their drinks.

A previous murder in the area had been found to have American connections and was thought to be the work of internationally organised crime. The MO of this latest murder also seemed to fit that brief. A hired assassin tracking his prey across the Atlantic before disappearing into the mists of mystery seemed the only conclusion. However, the body appeared to have been 'placed' and not dumped. The land was marshy so the victim must have been willing – or coerced – to walk with his murderer to the point of execution. It could also be concluded that the body was meant to be found, as it wasn't hidden down the pit-shaft, although the wall was over six feet high and would have been a difficult method of hiding the evidence.

George Rogers was brought in for questioning. Described as a shady character with many aliases, he was booking a ticket through an agency to America but was later grudgingly released by the authorities through lack of evidence to link him to the crime.

So what of Kent Reeks? The case went cold. The coroner's verdict could only be one of murder by assailants unknown.

The horror that greeted that young girl on that misty January morning must have stayed with her for the rest of her life. Four spent brass cartridge cases lay on the boggy ground close to the victim.

Two bullets had been shot through the victim's forehead, killing him immediately, and one bullet each for his eyes, supposedly to remove the image of the murderer, a ritual not seen in this country but one in keeping with gang executions in America.

FRIDAY THE 13TH VILLAGE SHOP MURDER AT LICKEY END

UPON HEARING NOISES DOWNSTAIRS IN THE EARLY MORNING HOURS MANY PEOPLE WOULD LEAVE THEIR WARM BEDS TO INVESTIGATE, ONLY TO FIND JUST A GUILTY-LOOKING CAT OR DOG. UNFORTUNATELY, FOR ONE OLD GENTLEMAN THIS WAS NOT THE CASE. INSTEAD, HE FOUND A FRENCHMAN WITH MALICIOUS INTENT SEARCHING HIS ROOM, HAVING ALREADY DELIVERED A FATAL BLOW.

These days Lickey End finds itself just south of the M42 motorway where the urban sprawl of Birmingham yields to the slightly more rural setting of the city's southern extent. This quiet spot in the January of 1893 was served by the main route of the Alcester Road, but disquiet was not far away at the small village of Long Eye.

Imagine an elderly couple making their living from a small village shop selling basic provisions. Joe and

Charlotte Pearcey were both in their seventies and relatively new to their roles in the village. Joe was worn out physically by manual labour, so he and Charlotte decided to set up a shop to sell groceries and other household provisions to the locals.

Life was still tough but a good deal cosier as Charlotte cooked Joe's breakfast and he snatched a couple of extra minutes in his warm bed on this Friday 13th. He was brought to his senses by a muffled scream and the sound of a struggle downstairs, followed by a heavy footfall on the stairs. Joe stayed as still as he could as he watched an intruder rifling through Charlotte's effects box at the foot of the bed. Joe then made a move, startling the robber who now realised he was being watched. So shocked was he that his scarf dropped from his face as his lifted a club to beat old Joe senseless.

The would-be attacker halted as cartwheels and horseshoes clattered on the cobbles outside. They brought an uneasy pause in proceedings. Neither victim nor thief wanted to make a sound or the first move. Joe had recognised the man, who suddenly took off down the stairs, banging the front door to as he went. The shop bell dutifully rang. Old Joe got himself out of bed and slowly made his way downstairs to meet the horror that greeted him. The smell of warm blood rose above the smell of his breakfast as Charlotte lay on the floor, mortally wounded. Joe ran out into the street crying *'Murder'* and soon the local policeman was calling for superiors to deal with this rare and brutal crime. Joe told the police that the man had been in his shop a few days earlier trying to sell items to Charlotte, who would have nothing to do with the sale. The man had pointed to a sign to say he was both deaf and dumb. Charlotte later joked with Joe that she had to see him off with a broom's tail from the shop.

A great effort from the police tracked the murder suspect to a house in Great Colmore Street, but his wife confirmed he had left the country. The honest salesman who was trying to work around his disability turned out to be a violent Frenchman who was a hawker of goods. He was named as Amie Holman Meunier, who lived with his English wife in Birmingham, and later when the assailant was interviewed he said he had faked being deaf and dumb to disguise the fact that he was French (the Napoleonic Wars were still strong in the collective memory then); the English would have hated him knowing he was French but they may have had sympathy for him if he was disabled. He even argued that the riots in Birmingham that had been inspired by the 1791 French Revolution were another reason not to show off his French nationality, as class division would have had him 'trodden underfoot!'

Birmingham and Bromsgrove Police managed to have him extradited from Belgium and at Worcester Assizes in the July of 1893 he faced a charge of murder. At his trial the Frenchman made only enemies of the court and the people. His torrents of questions and interjections even had the defence counsel at odds with him. For someone who traded on not speaking he'd clearly found his voice and his educated eloquence made him even more of an enigma.

In the end, he was found guilty and faced the scaffold at Worcester Gaol on 19th July. The prison bells rang that morning and the execution march began but even when the executioner placed the noose about the murderer's head he still had to have the last word. Suddenly, the man who had claimed he could not speak found his tongue again and said, *'Wait a bit, I am not dead yet!'* He went on to thank those assembled and to tell everyone he was ready to die. Even as the noose tightened around his neck his was silenced in mid-sentence but was heard to say, *'Kill me the first time…'*. At precisely eight o'clock the trapdoor opened and the Frenchman spoke no more.

MAN DOWN! BOBBY MURDERED!

THE DUTY OF A POLICE OFFICER IS ALWAYS FRAUGHT WITH RISK AND DANGER, NEVER MORE SO THAN IN THE DARK VICTORIAN ALLEYWAYS AND PASSAGEWAYS ON THE CITY LIMITS. ALTHOUGH THIS PARTICULAR MURDER HAPPENED IN A MORE RURAL ENVIRONMENT, THE ROOTS OF ITS CAUSE WERE FIRMLY ENTRENCHED IN THE UNDERBELLY OF BIRMINGHAM.

On the bitterly cold morning of 28th February 1885, PC James Davies' mutilated body was discovered on Eagle Lane, Wythall. In modern times, Wythall lies on the Hollywood bypass, which becomes the Alcester Road and now sits between two golf courses in the greenbelt area of land to the south of Birmingham. However, the scene was very different in late Victorian times, when the city limits streets were paved with pestilence and poverty and like rats from barrels the criminal element (either through desire or need), desperate for food, would run to the places where affluence and farming might bring them in a pretty penny or a meal – at whatever cost.

The trail of clues to the culprit would eventually lead investigators to those poor back streets of Brum where law and order were in as short a supply as food in a desperate person's belly.

Farm labourer John Twigg was heard shouting *'Murder!'* at the top of his voice by PC Whitehouse, who was jolted from his slumbers that morning. Quickly, he readied himself for what lay ahead. We can only imagine what thoughts must have gone through the mind of PC Whitehouse when he came across the body of his friend and colleague PC Davies. Putting his own feelings to one side, an investigation of the crime scene showed two sets of footprints behind the body leading back to a farmyard where the farmer reported that six hens were missing.

The body of his thirty-three-year-old colleague bore multiple knife wounds, inflicted by a man not just wishing to frighten or injure but one seemingly settling a score that had been a long time in coming. The only person who fitted this bill in mind of the police was poacher and long-time criminal Moses Shrimpton. As he was already known to the police for previous violent crimes and theft a photograph was issued for his arrest and soon he was traced to a hovel in Bartholomew Street, Birmingham, by officers from Duke Street police station.

Moses lived with another character of Brum's backstreets, long-serving prostitute and criminal 'Mad' Mary Morton. Shrimpton had returned the previous night covered in blood. A long-bladed knife was also found in the suspect's trademark tools. Maybe he thought Mary might give him a cover story through some unspoken criminal code. He was wrong. She was obviously trying to get into the police's good books and gave him no alibi, even though bloodstained blades were found in her skirts. In fact, she damned him by saying he had been out all night and confirming that he had returned in this state. Mad Mary said that after breakfast she had found her man scrubbing blood from his billycock (a hat similar to a tall bowler).

It could be argued that Moses was himself a victim, of poverty and the criminal system. He also had a liking for poaching and a hatred of the law. In fact, only a few hours before the murder, Shrimpton had refused to have his photograph taken outside The Swan pub with the victim of the murder and others connected with the hostelry.

Shrimpton's life and his behaviour at Winson Green gaol had left him hunched and bow-legged from the punishment of the treadwheel and the crank. His lifestyle had left him gaunt and thin. The crank was used as a punishment within the prison. The prisoner's penalty for bad behaviour was to turn the 'crank' for food. The prisoner would be given so many turns to earn food. The crank itself just turned wooden paddles in sandboxes, but the treadwheel was a different story. It was often used to power equipment in prisons. The prisoners worked shifts of ten minutes on and five minutes off for eight hours. Walking the wheel and turning the crank were seen as legal, wholesome punishments for the difficult prisoner in the Victorian prison.

The verdict of guilty of this heinous crime – brutally murdering a police officer merely for challenging a suspect for stealing chickens – ultimately carried the death penalty. The plaster casts of footprints that PC Whitehouse took at the scene of the crime, an example of early forensic work, matched the criminal's footwear and so damned him to the noose.

At 65 years of age, Moses Shrimpton finally met his fate at Worcester on 25th May 1885. His frenzied attack against the system, carried out on a representative of the law, held one final blow for Moses. James Berry, the hangman, who earned ten pounds a neck, got Shrimpton's weight wrong. The drop wasn't clean and decapitated the old poacher, which fortunately the witnesses did not see. Moses Shrimpton was one of 134 prisoners that were hanged by James Berry in his eight years as public executioner.

Mad Mary was released after being found not guilty of being an accessory to murder. PC James Davies left behind his heavily pregnant wife and four children and now lies in peace at St. Leonard's Church, Beoley. James Berry later made his fortune in America on lecture tours.

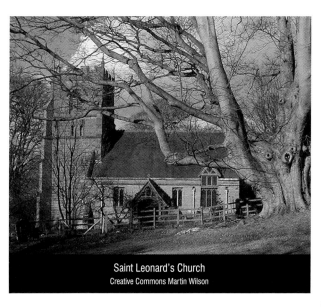

Saint Leonard's Church
Creative Commons Martin Wilson

FLIRTATIOUS FARM GIRL KILLS LOVER

IN THE EARLY EIGHTEENTH CENTURY THE RURAL AREAS TO THE SOUTH OF BIRMINGHAM PRESENTED WHAT MUST HAVE BEEN AN IDYLLIC 'CHOCOLATE BOX' SETTING. WORK WOULD HAVE BEEN CONFINED TO FARMS AND VILLAGES WITH EXCURSIONS TO MARKET. IT WAS A FEAST DAY MARKET THAT LED ONE YOUNG LADY INTO THE RECORDED HISTORY OF EXECUTION.

Catharine Hall was born in 1690 to a tenant farming family on the outskirts of the then small town of Birmingham. Little did society know that an infamous woman of questionable repute was about to be unleashed on an unsuspecting public. Catharine lived in the time before heavy industries had tainted the air and had drawn people into the urban squalor that would grow up in parts of Birmingham and the Black Country.

Although poor, her family would go to the Birmingham Horse Fair that was held twice a year at Whit and

Michaelmas. The fair itself consisted of traders in all sorts of goods and wares, and livestock sales were held in and around the Bull Ring area of the city. When she was thirteen years of age, she went to her first fair and was taken in by the noise and the colour of the proceedings.

A paper reporting on Catharine poeticaly described her as *'A wilful wench with roving eye, made feyther [father] rage an' mother sigh.'* On one trip to Brum a couple of years later, she caught the eye of an army officer who persuaded her to come and live with him at the army camp. In no time she was a popular lady with access to the whole of the officers' mess. Her escapades finally led to her removal from the camp. Now branded a scarlet woman, she was unable to return to her past life and embrace once more the values held dear within her home community.

She set off through Warwickshire with no place to go, but fortuitously found work as a servant girl in the employ of a simple farming family. Here she quickly 'fell' for John Hayes, a carpenter and the oldest son of the family, and soon they were secretly married. Flighty Catharine, though, became disillusioned with her simple life yet again and talked her husband into moving to London, where they would seek their fortune as money-lenders. They could use what money he had to set them up in business.

Unfortunately, whatever success they had in business was about to turn ugly. John resented the overbearing nature of his wife and their relationship started to become one of arguments. Catharine soon came to the conclusion that her husband needed to be silenced. One day, two lodgers appeared at their door. Tom Billings was introduced to John as her brother but in fact was an old flame from Brum, while the other man was a Mr Wood. Catharine had twelve children by this time and now boasted three lovers!

As Billings and Wood were accepted into the marital home on the Oxford Road in Tyburn, Kate's plan unfolded. Tom challenged John to a drinking bout and so it was that, on 1st March 1725, in a drunken stupor, John Hayes had a hatchet cleaved into his skull by Tom Billings. On hearing terrible cries, a neighbour rushed round to see if everything was all right. Kate, as she called herself, simply said she would ask her guests to make less noise. Tom found himself sickened by the scene and the sight of blood, as John didn't die quickly but continued to roam around the room. To save further mess, Catharine held her husband's head over a bucket, whilst Tom removed John's head with a large knife. Finally, John succumbed to the onslaught and the house went quiet.

Once more, Catharine took charge and Billings was now completely controlled by her and at her mercy. She ordered him to hide the head under his coat and go and lose it in the River Thames. Unfortunately for Billings, the tide was out and he had to wade through the mud to fling the bloody package into the water. A tramp, however, had witnessed his actions and went to retrieve the parcel after Billings had left. The horror that befell the poor witness on untying the parcel led him to start shouting *'Murder!'*

The poor wretch was quickly found by the Parish Officers, who promptly cleaned the head up and mounted it on a stake before displaying it for identification purposes at St. Margaret's in Westminster. After many a person had filed past, finally someone recognised the features of John Hayes and promptly ran to tell Catharine the news. During this time, she and Billings were readying the victim's body to be scattered in a pond on Marylebone Fields. Catharine turned the messenger away and threatened them with legal action for spreading malicious lies.

Catharine and Billings moved to another address and carried on the money-lending business, though the suspicions of the authorities had now been aroused and the couple were being watched. On 24th March, the body of John Hayes was recovered from the murky watery shroud that had hidden him. Catharine and Billings were found in bed by the authorities and Wood was arrested for his part in the unlawful proceedings.

Catharine protested her innocence and unsuccessfully tried to poison herself on hearing the execution date of 9th May. Wood died in Newgate Prison and Billings was sentenced to be hanged. Catharine, however, was to meet her fate at the stake rather than the noose in view of her barbaric and unseemly nature.

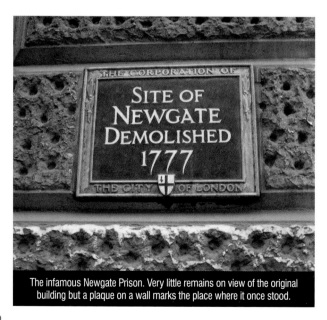

THE CORPORATION OF

SITE OF NEWGATE DEMOLISHED 1777

THE CITY OF LONDON

The infamous Newgate Prison. Very little remains on view of the original building but a plaque on a wall marks the place where it once stood.

As was the legal process then, the executioner would render the accused unconscious through strangulation before the fires were lit. However, this procedure was thwarted by an early match being applied to the tinder, leaving 'Killer Kate' alive and at the mercy of the flames. Her screams rang out as onlookers threw pieces of wood at her. One piece hit her squarely on the head and killed her outright.

One thing is for certain, and that is that a simple visit to the Horse Fair ultimately changed the lives and led to the deaths of so many people. It also changed the law of the land, as she was the last woman to be burned alive for petty treason, a fact that made the Brummy 'Killer Kate' notorious in more ways than one.

Her story went on to be told in part by William Makepeace Thackeray in the story of *Catherine*, serialised in *Fraser's Magazine* in 1839 and 1840, and in the 1950s her story became a radio play.

HORSELESS HIGHWAYMAN CONVICTION

THE FAMILIAR ROMANTIC FIGURE OF A BOLD HIGHWAYMAN PROUDLY ASTRIDE HIS NOBLE STEED COULDN'T BE FURTHER FROM THE TRUTH IN THIS STORY OF A COWARDLY MURDER BY A MAN OF THE ROADS AND A BULLET IN THE BACK OF HIS ELDERLY VICTIM RETURNING FROM MARKET.

'You rascal!' retorted farmer Benjamin Robins, as he felt the warm trickle of blood running down his back. He knew he had been shot as the dull percussive thud had struck a split second earlier, lodging the invasive lead slug in his body. The bullet was later removed, having entered the middle of his back and travelled over a foot through the body to where it finally halted its fatal path.

It was the evening of 18th December 1812 and Robins was walking home to Dunsley Hall, Kinver, from Stourbridge market. He had only another half-mile to go to safety, but fate intervened that evening on Dunsley Heath. The freshly fallen snow turned red as Robins called out to his attacker, informing him that he hadn't needed to shoot. Robins staggered the half-mile after being relieved of his valuables and left a trail of blood up the staircase on reaching the Hall.

Dunsley Hall, built in an area rich in history
Creative Commons Gordon Griffiths

Robins described his attacker later that evening to two attendant surgeons who tried to stem the flow of blood from his wound. The farmer had got a clear view of the robber and went on to say he was well dressed with a good hat, wore a dark coat and walked with a wide gait.

At the Angel public house in Stourbridge that evening, at around six o'clock, a man sat drinking quietly in the corner, keeping himself to himself and listening to the outrage of the locals reporting on the story of a farmer returning from market only to be robbed in his own neighbourhood. One went on to say that the shot had not found its mark and that Robins could make a recovery. That same man had earlier that day taken a lunch of a pork pie and a quart of ale in the *Nag's Head* public house, where the landlord had commented on the man's attire.

William Howe, described by some as a highwayman without a horse, was that day intent on getting transport and cash. He eyed one potential victim, Compton farmer Thomas Bates, with a menacing expression. Bates, who later went on to identify Howe, saying that he had never seen a *'more evil pair of eyes in his life'*, escaped his gaze by geeing his horse on to get away.

And so it was at Fir Tree Hill – soon to be given a more evocative name, as we shall see – that witnesses saw Howe give determined chase to his quarry, but no one saw the crime. That night Howe booked himself into Stourbridge's Duke William Hotel and stayed there until eight the following morning.

Doctor Causer attended to Robins for the next ten

days until finally the victim succumbed to his wound and died on 28th December. Immediately, justice was called for from his friends and neighbours. Stourbridge magistrates requested the assistance of Bow Street Runners Sam Taunton and Harry Adkins. Both men were seen as excellent detectives and they went about their business gathering information on the suspect. Local stories led the pair to Ombersley, where on 22nd December Howe had packed his bags and was now going under the alias of John Wood. They also discovered that two boxes had been dispatched by the man, who had then left for London. Quickly, the 'Runners' left for the address on the boxes, *The Castle and Falcon Inn* on Aldersgate Street, London.

Howe was arrested and returned to Stourbridge to face the charges, but he denied the crime, stating that although he had been in Stourbridge at the time he neither knew the victim or had heard of his unfortunate circumstances, saying that his heart was innocent. Unfortunately for Howe, the magistrates saw otherwise and accepted that there was enough evidence for Howe to stand trial.

As Howe awaited his fate he smuggled a letter to his visiting wife, telling her to search a hayrick in Stourbridge and remove the incriminating evidence that lay there. The letter was intercepted by the authorities, who arranged a search and found a pistol and three lead shot. Pistols usually came in pairs at this time and the pistol found in Stourbridge matched the pistol found at an associated address in London by the 'Runners'. Also, Robins' watch was recovered from a pawnbrokers in Warwick and had been left by a man matching Howe's description. The evidence was now stacking up beyond reasonable doubt.

Howe was found guilty of murder and sentenced to hang; and further, to hang at the location of his crime. From the scaffold Howe admitted his guilt and warned others not to follow in his footsteps. Howe's body, clad in irons, was removed from Stafford Gaol on 18th March 1813 following his execution at the 'new drop', as it was called at Stafford. The next day his body was suspended from a tree on Fir Tree Hill – now renamed Gibbet Lane – near to the place where he had confronted Mr Robins as a lesson to other would-be highway entrepreneurs.

In 1903 a skeleton was unearthed at the site. The skeleton had a knife in its ribcage. If this was the remains of Howe it follows that a superstition from the time had been invoked, as it was believed that a dagger pushed through the heart of a criminal stopped the soul from rising above ground. He was not meant to ever get away!

CHIEF WITNESS? THE VICTIM!

DOMESTIC VIOLENCE IN VICTORIAN BRITAIN WAS UNFORTUNATELY A REGULAR OCCURRENCE. FED BY POVERTY AND DRINK, IT OFTEN LED TO GREATER CRIMES AND VIOLENCE AS WHAT WENT ON BEHIND FRONT DOORS WAS DEEMED TO BE NO BUSINESS OF ANYONE ELSE'S. BLIND BOOZE-RIDDEN ANGER OFTEN BURNED BACK TO REMORSE, BUT IN THIS CASE IT WAS SADLY TOO LATE.

'He said, "Give me a kiss, Polly." Then he, my husband, murdered me.' Polly was clinging to life when she managed to report details of her murder to a magistrate. She told of when and how before finally succumbing to the extent of her wounds.

A statement or, as it was known then, a deposition, was recorded in writing by Mr Bowen, Clerk to Bilston Magistrates, in July 1860. Sitting at the victim's bedside he recorded the details as life ebbed away from the poor victim.

Mary 'Polly' Twigg was no stranger to domestic violence. Her husband, Samuel Twigg, thirty-five years old and a bricklayer from Bilston, was a drinker and had a history of beating her. When sober he later admitted that he had no reason to kill or even show violence to his wife, who he told the court 'was as good as ever broke a piece of bread'.

It appears that Samuel Twigg suffered from mood swings and pains in the head. His son, giving evidence at Stafford Assizes, said that his father had been struck on the head with a policeman's truncheon during a previous bout of drunkenness and had suffered from the pains from then on. In times of drunken bravado Samuel Twigg would boast that he was the 'Cock of the Walk', meaning no one could best him. When he was in these moods Polly would have to 'get out of his road', and so it was on 25th July 1860 when Mary Twigg recorded her witness statement of how she was murdered. At eleven o'clock that very evening Mary lay still in a pool of her own blood, fatally stabbed through the liver and her husband duly arrested for her murder.

In Mary's deposition, recorded in the absence of her husband, though he was restrained in another room, she tells the story of her husband returning home in a drunken state with a drinking buddy. They made so much noise she got out of bed and, dressed in nothing but her nightdress, she let them in. She argued with the other man that he should go back to his wife but he would not leave and said he had no wife. Mary went upstairs to put her shawl and chemise on, to the cussing and cursing of her irate husband. He threatened to cut her head off at one point if she didn't come back downstairs.

Eventually the other man left after Samuel Twigg threatened to cut Mary's throat 'from ear to ear' if she didn't cook some steaks. After more cursing, Samuel Twigg called Mary to make a light for him so he could go to bed. As she took a light from the coal fire to do so, Samuel Twigg drew his knife, flicked it open and viciously stabbed Mary in the side as she turned towards him. Mary felt the blood swell beneath her hand and quickly ran to a neighbour opposite. Mrs Walton, a relative through marriage who lived on the other side of the courtyard properties in Coseley Row, took Mary in and made her comfortable and at two in the morning Dr Larkin was called to administer treatment. He knew she had been mortally wounded and couldn't do anything to save her.

In judgment at the Assizes on 17th December Samuel Twigg was found guilty of murder and sentenced to hang. A petition was raised for the sentence to be one of penal servitude. However, the judge said the sentence stood as drunkenness was no excuse for committing murder.

On 4th January 1861 at 8a.m. a crowd of three thousand people saw Samuel Twigg stand at the gallows. He had walked unaided, though it is reported that he stumbled before the hood and rope were put in place. As the clock bell chimed, Samuel Twigg took the drop and died instantly, and was buried in the grounds of Stafford Gaol.

Stafford Gaol

Before his execution Twigg had left the prison chaplain a written confession to his crime. The sequence of events matched that of Mary's deposition. In addition, he admitted to verbally abusing her as she toasted some bacon for him. She had turned and shaken him in response just before the knife was plunged into her body.

The Twiggs' sixteen-year-old son remembered his father buying the knife two weeks before the murder. The police found the weapon in the dying ashes of the fire. It still bore the price ticket of one shilling.

A BAKER AND HIS SECRETS

THE OLD ROMAN TOWN OF SMALL HEATH LIES TO THE SOUTH-EAST OF BIRMINGHAM. THIS SMALL TRADE TOWN SITS ON A HILL AND ITS RECENT CLAIM TO FAME IS BEING PART OF THE SETTING FOR THE BRUMMY GANGLAND TELEVISION SERIES *PEAKY BLINDERS*, WHICH SUGGESTS SOMETHING OF WHAT THE TOWN WAS LIKE DURING THE INTER-WAR YEARS.

On 17th February 1907 the *Birmingham Echo* reported on an incident that caused great interest amongst the locals as the horrific findings made in a small property led to a story that spread around the tight-knit community and went on to prove that fact is often stranger than fiction.

A baker routinely went out on his rounds every day around mid-morning delivering his produce to the many regular local stops he had built up over the years. This would have led to him gaining a great knowledge of the comings and goings of people on his round. However, all this changed when on this fateful day he knocked on the door of 27 Byron Road at around midday. He waited a while and knocked again, but no one, it seems, was there to open the door. The baker became concerned when nobody replied, as this was very unusual for this particular family. His concerns grew to something of a more serious nature and he then began to fear the worst.

He hurriedly left the property and immediately went to summon the local police officer, Sergeant Holland, who attended the scene straight away. After a few minutes of knocking on the door and listening out for movement within the premises it became apparent that if anyone was in the house they had clearly been incapacitated in some way. Eventually, access was gained to the premises via a window and, after an examination of the house, the officer made the unfortunate find of two dead bodies, one man and one woman. Looking around him and noting their injuries he saw that the lady had suffered severe head injuries and the man a nasty cut to his throat.

Doctor Notley was called in to examine the bodies before their removal to the mortuary and established that both were indeed extinct of life. The doctor also observed that they had not been dead long and estimated that they had died sometime during the previous evening. Further investigations by the police led to the finding of a bloodstained hammer and a bloody razor in the same room and in the vicinity of the bodies.

It transpired that the couple had been at this address for around ten years. Mr Turner was aged sixty and worked as a foreman mechanic and, as far as people understood, kept himself to himself. The lady was much more of a mystery and was only seen on occasion, as both led a very private and quiet existence.

When questioned, neighbours reported that the lady was rarely seen out and about and when she was seen outside of the house she always wore a very thick, dark veil, which some believed to be hiding a facial disfigurement of some sort. No one knew where the couple had come from and no one had heard a sound that night. Not a sound, a scream or a thud as two people decided that life was too painful. Their demise was considered just as mysterious as their arrival in this small town.

It appears from the findings and the subsequent report that Mr Turner avoided both the trial and the noose by first killing the lady in his life and then cutting his own throat. No conclusion was reported upon in the press as far as can be seen and much remains open to conjecture. Was this a suicide pact that had such a brutal ending? Was it a crime of compassion and deep love? Was the lady's disfigurement too much to bear, resulting in both deciding to take their lives by Mr Turner killing his wife and then himself? Was Mr Turner a brutal man? Was the mysterious veil perhaps required to mask facial injuries that Mr Turner had himself bestowed upon his partner?

One thing that is a certainty is that Mr Turner was guilty of both murder and suicide. This particular incident was a true open-and-shut case for detectives. But what drove this quiet, mysterious couple into such violent actions and such a fatal decision? The answer died that day with Mr Turner and the mysterious veiled lady in his life.

THE MOON AND THE MODERN-DAY WEREWOLF

A MODERN-DAY WEREWOLF KNOWN AS THE 'MOON KILLER' FELT THE TIDES IN HIS MIND SHIFT ONE FATEFUL NIGHT IN 1950, BUT ON THIS OCCASION IT LED HIM TO HIS DARK SIDE, SOMETHING TO WHICH HE WAS NO STRANGER. UNFORTUNATELY FOR HIS VICTIM IT LED HIM TO HER BEDSIDE.

In March 1950 Birmingham CID was called in to investigate a suspicious death at 108 Hingeston Street, Brookfields, a densely occupied street of small terraced houses whose front doors led directly onto the pavement. The street is in close proximity to the Jewellery Quarter, lying to the west of the area with Icknield Street being the divisive ribbon between the two areas of Birmingham.

Elsie Ivy Aston, a fifty-seven-year-old lady, was found dead in bed by her daughter, Ivy Watkins, on 30th March 1950. Ivy lived in a nearby house and it was usual for her to visit her mother early in the morning to help with the housework before she went off to work. It was also a bit of company for Mrs Aston, as she had been a widow for four years. Mrs Aston was described as a friendly person with quite a few friends but lived a quiet life. She occasionally went out for a drink with friends and relatives but in the main kept herself to herself and worked in Birmingham. Mrs Aston had been out drinking in Hockley the night before and was witnessed to still have been alive at around half past ten that night by her sister-in-law. She had walked Mrs Aston to her door and heard the lock click behind her, so she knew her relative was 'safe' at home.

At around 5.50 a.m. a door was heard being slammed shut in the vicinity of the house in which Mrs Aston's body was found. The police accepted that this would have been the approximate time of death. Mrs Aston was found in her bedroom on the first floor with what were described at the time as 'marks' to her body.

Professor Webster carried out the post-mortem on the same day to find out the actual cause of death, but back at the property the news had spread and pandemonium ensued in the street. The CID and uniformed police were coming and going from the property and the sight of this led to the police then having to manage the crowd of hundreds of onlookers of all ages swarming the streets. They were waiting to see Ivy Watkins returning to her mother's address after giving a statement at the station. Plain-clothes officers were also seen removing Mrs Aston's bedclothes from the scene, 'all bundled up and tied off with string'.

The officers had come to the conclusion of foul play following the discovery of a piece of broken cast iron grating which fed air into the cellar to help keep it dry. This was seen as the forced point of entry to the property and they concluded that the assailant could have spent time hiding in the house.

You may well be wondering why such an ignition of interest had taken place after the discovery of Mrs Aston's body. To understand why the police had mobilised so quickly we need to turn the clock back eighteen months.

Harriet Mills, a sixty-nine-year-old lady, was found dead in bed at the neighbouring property in Hingeston Street. Harriet was also found with marks to her body. Professor Webster had examined the body of Harriet Mills in October 1948 and had ruled out natural causes, concluding that death had occurred 'through the manual constriction of the neck', but the jury at the time gave an 'accidental death' decision to the inquest. The order was given to look at both sets of files of the deceased ladies, as the police tried to tie the evidence of the two deaths together.

After the death of Mrs Aston, the police asked for witnesses to step forward who might have seen a person leaving the house with bloodstained hands and clothing and possibly catching the early morning bus with workers going about their normal business.

The following day thirty-four-year-old baker's assistant Alan Dennis Witcomb was arrested for the murder of Mrs Aston, his address given as number 1 – the back of 120 – Hingeston Street. He admitted to being in the property of Mrs Aston but couldn't remember a thing other than that. Witcomb had admitted to his sister that *'the moon did strange things to him'*. It was argued at the Stipendiary Court, where Lord Ilkeston requested the accused to take his hands out of his pockets, that Mrs Aston would have received the wounds from which she died at the hands of the man now standing in the dock.

No one could have predicted the revelations that were to eventually come out of this case. Witcomb admitted killing Harriet Mills, a similar situation of the moon shining and an inability to sleep leading him to strangle or suffocate his victims before himself passing out on the bed next to them. A statement followed from DI Evans, made years earlier regarding the death of Witcomb's niece, whom the defendant said he had suffocated in 1933. A doctor's report gave evidence that the child had stopped breathing due to a blockage and so Witcomb had not been arrested.

Witcomb described his actions as 'sudden urges' and when giving a statement to police regarding the death of Harriet Mills said, *'I did her, I squeezed her neck. I'll be happier when things are cleared up.'* He did not, however, admit to his guilt in court and at Birmingham Assizes was defended on the grounds of insanity. When all the evidence was given, Witcomb was found guilty and sentenced to Broadmoor. Three cases were thus resolved and the general public were now safe from the self-confessed 'Moon Killer'.

Hingeston Street showing densely packed terraced houses
Creative Commons

LADY KILLER SWINGS AT WINSON GREEN

OUR NEXT CASE HAS VERY LIMITED INFORMATION THAT CAN BE GLEANED FROM THE MANY RESOURCES AT OUR FINGERTIPS TODAY. MUCH OF THE STORY INVOLVES SOME LEVEL OF SUPPOSITION BUT THE OUTCOME WAS JUST AS GRISLY AS MANY WELL-DOCUMENTED MURDERS. THE REASON FOR ITS INCLUSION IS FOR ITS REGIONAL SOCIAL IMPORTANCE AS MUCH AS THE HORRIFIC SUBJECT OF MURDER.

It seems a fairly modern arrangement, something that would go unnoticed today: two people living together free from the bounds and perceived constraints of marriage, where a couple can have a purely contractual approach to the domestic arrangements and finances relating to shared goods and wealth (or debt for that matter) that accrue throughout a long-term relationship.

This story, however, is not a modern-day romance or the tale of a pre-nuptial agreement turning sour and ending in tragedy. It is one of a post-relationship contract and one for which we have to turn the clocks back to a

December day in 1874 when a Birmingham couple, who had been living together for seventeen years, decided to finally call it a day on their time together. On Christmas Day 1884 Henry Kimberley and Harriet Stewart looked at their combined standing in society and recorded that they had a house, a piano and £20 in savings. Henry's love for Harriet may well have clouded his judgement on the subjective issue of who got what from the dissolution of domestic arrangements. Henry agreed that Harriet should keep the house and he would take the piano and the £20.

The agreement had been a mutual one and seemingly without remorse or regret up until the dawning of the realisation of what they had done. Henry was reported to have immediately asked Harriet to scrap the contract and for them to resume their life together. Harriet's reply, apparently, was a curt one, being quoted as *'What's yours is yours and what's mine is mine!'*

Within two days, the decision to separate from Harriet, combined with her rebuttal towards him, must have sent Henry Kimberley into an emotional turmoil. Whether Henry had been following his ex or whether the meeting that followed was pure fate we may never know but it bought the powerful emotions of love and jealousy, heartbreak and pain to The White Hart Inn in the centre of Birmingham.

Harriet had been seen by Kimberley entering the hostelry with her friend Mrs Emma Palmer, wife of Thomas. Immediately, Kimberley saw the opportunity to try to win back the affections of his long-time lover once more. Kimberley approached the two women and confronted them firstly with a request for Harriet to return to his arms. She emphatically rejected his offer with a simple *'No!'* Kimberley then turned to Harriet's friend Emma and begged her to persuade Harriet to come back to him. In the tense silence that followed the barman and some customers were becoming aware of a potential situation. Emma shook her head defiantly and stood by her friend's decision. Kimberley went on to say that he still loved Harriet, but none of his remonstrations gleaned any solace from the two ladies. Torn apart and clearly emotional, Kimberley pulled out a gun and cleanly shot both ladies at what must have been very close quarters.

Immediately, the barman raced over to wrestle the gun from Kimberley, who took a shot at him but was unsuccessful in making his getaway, as the barman, aided by several customers, restrained the potential murderer until the police were summoned to the bloody scene.

The two women lay wounded on the floor of the inn as Kimberley was taken to the station under arrest for his crime. Harriet survived her ex's attempt to kill her.

Kimberley must have been of the mind to think that if he couldn't have her no one else could. Unfortunately, Emma succumbed to her wounds after twelve days of battling for her life in hospital.

Kimberley was held in gaol before finally he faced the charge of murder at the February sessions of the Birmingham Assizes. Once all the evidence had been heard, he was found guilty of murder and sentenced to hang for his crimes. He duly met the executioner and the noose on the morning of Tuesday 17th March 1885, the gallows being set at Birmingham's Winson Green Prison. Kimberley not only had his life terminated that day for a crime of passion but he also went into the records as the first execution there since 1802. Thomas Palmer buried his wife in the grounds of St. Mary's Church, Acock's Green. She died on 8th January 1885, at only 37 years of age.

BIBLIOGRAPHY

BOOKS

COCHRANE, DON, *Black Country Murders*
JONES, STEVE, *Birmingham… The Sinister Side*
LETHBRIDGE, J.P, *Murder In The Midlands*
MORGAN, VANESSA, *Murder and Crime in Birmingham*
PARSONS, HAROLD, *Murder and Mystery in The Black Country*

ARCHIVES

Birmingham Central Library
Black Country Bugle

NEWSPAPERS

Birmingham Gazette
Birmingham Daily Press
Birmingham Evening Dispatch
Birmingham and Aston Chronicle
The Birmingham Weekly Post
The Birmingham Echo
The Birmingham News
The Birmingham Bugle
The Black Country Bugle

WEBSITES

Wikipedia
www.blackcountrymuse.com
www.dunsleyhallhotel.co.uk
www.truecrimelibrary.com
www.birminghammail.co.uk